Biff couldn't sleep.

Dad told her a story.

The story was about a dragon.

Biff dreamed about the dragon.

It was a nasty dragon.

It was a very nasty dragon.

Biff had to fight it.

Biff went downstairs.

Mum told her a story.

The story was about a dolphin.

Biff dreamed about a dolphin.